I0405350

Selling Your North Shore Home

How to Get Maximum ROI When You Decide to Move

Kenny MacCarthy

Selling Your North Shore Home

Printed by:
90-Minute Books
302 Martinique Drive
Winter Haven, FL 33884
www.90minutebooks.com

Published in the United States of America

140906-001.2

ISBN-13: 978-1503060524
ISBN-10: 1503060527

Here's What's Inside…

Selling Your North Shore Home!

August, 2017
Beverly Farms, MA

Very few people look forward to selling their home, especially if they've lived in it for any length of time. It's a hassle; packing up decades worth of belongings, finding an agent, legal paperwork, organizing a move. Never mind the emotional toll. It's a daunting project.

Since becoming an agent over 20 years ago, I've had the opportunity to work with hundreds of people who have bought and sold homes on the North Shore. My clients and their individual situations have taught me so much. Specifically, what works and what doesn't. This insight is priceless.

Being able to share this message is important to me so I asked professional interviewer Susan Austin to help capture my thoughts and bring them together in this book. What follows is a conversation you can join in with as I share my observations and experiences on how to avoid the mistakes made by others; how to ultimately get the best price possible for your property with the most efficient use of your time and resources.

In this book, I'll explain some simple tasks that can make you thousands of dollars, including how a well-timed visit to the assessor's office can exponentially boost your buyer's perception of value. I also answer common questions such as:

When is the right time to put our North Shore home on the market? At what price? How do we find the right people to help us?

I hope you find this book enlightening. There are a lot of misconceptions in the marketplace that cause a lot of missed opportunities and money left on the table. If you know the process before you dive in, you'll have a much more satisfying experience. My systems works. I'm happy to share it with you and make your life a little bit easier.

To Your Success!

Kenny MacCarthy

Why Do Some North Shore Homes Sell Faster than Others?

Susan: I'm excited to have the opportunity to talk with you Kenny, and help share your thoughts and ideas on selling a home on the North Shore.

Let's start with why you think some North Shore homes sell faster than others?

Kenny: It usually comes down to the preparation that's done prior to going on the market. Most sellers don't perform nearly enough of it because they don't realize their property needs it. To them, their "home" is priceless; it's where they raised their kids, celebrated birthdays, played with the dog. It's home. It's priceless and perfect.

But the market doesn't consider it priceless. Buyers see a box on a street, not a home. They see the numbers, not the emotions. So, sellers have to make several really important decisions before they put the house up for sale.

Why do some sell faster than others? It's the preparation and getting the appropriate people involved right from the start.

I'm looking forward to sharing here, all the things that you can do well in advance, as well as what to do just before you are ready to list the property for sale.

Susan: So let's assume I'm thinking about selling my home here on the North Shore. How far out should I be looking to start to prepare for selling my home?

Kenny: It all depends on your living situation. If you are in a job where you move every four or five years, then you should be thinking two or three years out. If you are in a situation where you're going to be there for the next 10 years or 15 years, I would say start thinking about it three or four years before you are getting ready to sell.

The maintenance of a home is key. I see many homes where the seller will call me and say, "Come tell me what I need to do to my property to get it ready to go on the market." They've lived in it for 15 years and haven't taken the time to maintain the home over those 15 years. That's going to cost them tens of thousands of dollars and there will still be maintenance can't be done in a reasonable time frame before it goes on the market. You need to chip away at the maintenance and keep up with it. Do the roof when it needs to be done. Remodel the kitchen. Remodel the bathrooms. Refinish the floors.

Keep up with repairs on your house. Today's buyer does not want to buy a property that is run down. They really don't want to move in and take on a project. They are looking for move in ready. If it is a project, it's going cost you tens of thousands of dollars. It sounds like common sense, but it never ceases to amaze me the number of people who just don't take care of their property while they are living in it. They get used to looking at the peeling paint. They get used to looking at the stained carpeting.

Long before you get ready to sell, have an agent come in and take a look at your house periodically to give you an idea. "How is my house looking?" "Does my house smell?" "What does it look like from the street?" I can't tell you how many times I've walked in to somebody's home and there's an odor. That means something is wrong. Get a fresh set of eyes on your property. And get a fresh nose.

This lack of preparation is sometimes just because people don't know what to do. They don't have a system in place. I have a booklet that I'm happy to send out. It's called *Tips to Help You Get Maximum Money*. There are some really straightforward tips in there that will get people thinking about ideas to get their property ready to go on the market and how to keep it maintained so that, when they are ready to put it on the market, it will look like a model home.

Buyers love model homes. They love walking into a property that has little or no maintenance necessary on it, that looks like it came out of a magazine, and they can just move right in and start using it. That's ideally what most buyers want. Think model home when you are getting ready.

Email me at **kenny@capeanninfo.com** and ask for *Tips to Help You Get Maximum Money* and I'll send it right out.

When Is the Right Time to Sell?

Susan: OK, I have my home in good shape, ready to put on the market. When is the right time for someone to sell their North Shore home?

Kenny: There are a couple of different ways to look at this. People often have emergencies, or so called "life events" which come up. People pass away, get divorced, find new jobs, and lose old jobs. Life events. Not easy to plan for especially when it necessitates selling the home.

That being said, the best time of year to sell, here on the North Shore, is springtime. When the plants are blooming, when the leaves are coming out, and that's late April or May for us.

Buyers start thinking about buying right after the Super Bowl. It's almost like they flip a switch and they start thinking, "Why don't we do something this year?" February is not the time to put the property on the market. There's still snow on the ground. Before Christmas, the snow looks good with the lights and all the "good will towards men". But January and February around here, I would not want to have my property on the market, unless I had a life event going on and I needed to sell it. And buyers know that. If you can wait, the best time to put it on the market would be springtime.

How to Figure out What Your North Shore Home Is Worth...

Susan: One of the first questions people must ask is about price. How can I figure out what my North Shore home is worth?

Kenny: There are several systematic ways that we use to determine the marketing price of a property. The first one I call "the appraiser's view." Since most sales are going to end up having a bank loan tied to the purchase, I think like an appraiser since the appraiser will make or break the sale when he/she says "OK. It's worth what they've agreed to pay. Lend them the money."

To get to this point, the appraiser must prove that the property is worth the agreed upon price. Let's use $750,000 for the sake of this example. To do this, the appraiser is going to look at "like, kind, and quality" of properties near the subject property. These "comps" must have been sold very recently. If it's a property in Manchester, they are going to look at only Manchester properties that are approximately the same size, built the same year, and about the same quality. They are also going to look at properties that have been sold in the last two to four months. They don't like to go back any further than that. With this information, the appraiser will come up with a value. That's "the appraiser's view".

We also need to take a look at the "assessor's view." The assessor, the tax person in the particular town, places a value on the property. Properties sell for a percentage of assessed value. In some communities, they sell for assessed value. In others, they sell for less than assessed. Here on the North Shore, over or under assessed is often determined by "is it on the water or not on the water?" Properties that are on the water sell for a substantially higher price than assessed value. Properties that have a water view also usually sell for higher than assessed value. The view factor is hard for the assessor to quantify. Right now, in our North Shore market, the assessed value is another good rule of thumb for what many properties are worth.

Here's a secret. Buyers don't like to pay more than assessed value. They are very savvy and aware and can go on-line and see what a property is worth, according to the assessor. One of the first things that will bother them, if your property is assessed at $700,000 but it's on the market for $800,000, they'll wonder, "Why is it more than the assessed value? The assessments around here are done every year. The assessors' software is actually very accurate." Buyers will want to know why it's higher than the assessed value.

So get the assessor to change the assessed value of your property. Call and make sure the assessor has the correct information about your property. Invite him/her to come over and see all of the improvements you've made over the years. They'll love it. No one EVER asks them to come over. We recommended this to clients last week. They are getting ready to sell and so we looked at the assessor's information. The assessor says, "It's a two bedroom house, 1,200 square feet." My clients have added a bedroom that the assessor doesn't know about, which automatically adds value to the property, so I recommended that they call and have the assessor come and look at their property and change that assessed value. The assessor will think you are crazy, but you won't be if you can add fifty, seventy-five, or a hundred thousand dollars to the assessed value of your property by the time you put it on the market. You will automatically raise the value in the buyer's mind and increase its market value.

Susan: That is a fantastic secret. So straight forward to do, but I imagine very few people actually know to do it.

If someone wants to know exactly how much their house is worth, is that a service you provide?

Kenny: Absolutely. We're happy to meet and "assess" your home.

There are also steps you can take yourself online. Every community here on the North Shore has a website. For example, it's Gloucesterma.gov, or Rockportma.gov, and you can get the assessed values right there. You can also get plot plans for your home. All this information is public knowledge. That's why it's so important to understand that people are going to find this information before they even look at your property, so you want to make sure that it's accurate.

Zillow is another reference that we use for pricing. It has become a benchmark in the real estate world. Buyers love Zillow. But many sellers say, "Oh my gosh, Zillow is wrong. My house is worth a lot more than that." Well, I have attended national seminars given by Zillow, and they admit they overvalue properties 15% of the time and they undervalue properties 15% of the time. 30% of the time, they are wrong, but Zillow is what we call a black box. They take information from many different sources and run it through their "black box" of algorithms to come up with a value. One of their biggest sources of information is a city's or town's assessor's database. So that's another great reason, if you've got some time before you are putting your property on the market, to call the assessor and have him/her make a visit to see if you can raise your assessed value.

How to Pick the Right People to Market Your Home...

Susan: Kenny, talk to me about picking the right agent. There is a lot of choice out there. What are the important things I should be looking for in an agent?

Kenny: I have written a white paper called *13 Steps on How to Find a Really Effective Agent*. It basically starts out with some communication exercises folks can use test and see if an agent is communicative. Step one is "search Google for real estate agents in, for example, Manchester, MA. Make a note of the agents on the first page. "Go to Zillow and look for the professionals," is step two. It goes on from there. I'm happy to share this white paper. It will help to identify the top four or five or six agents in the area. There are also scripts that you can use to send each one of these agents an email. It's best, at the initial search stage, to ask the same questions. Then you'll also be able to gauge how quickly each agent gets back to you.

My business is all about communication and right off the bat, if they are not communicating with you when you are looking for an agent, you don't want to be doing business with him/her. You're going to want updates all the time from the person that you pick. So, one of the things I recommend heavily in my *How to Find a Really Effective Agent* is the communication aspect and how quickly they respond. I also have a number of questions that you can ask the agent. It's important to ask the same questions of every agent so that you are comparing apples to apples. For example, "Do you work by yourself, or have a team? Describe the members of your team. Who works with buyers? Who works with sellers? If I hire you, would I be working with you, or one of your team members? If so, who in your team? How many buyer/seller clients are you and your team currently working with?"

Susan: Would you suggest I do this by email?

Kenny: Yes, start off via email and you will find out very quickly that, and I state this in the white paper, if people don't get back to you within 24 hours, you don't bother with them. If they aren't checking their email at least once a day, I don't want to do business with them. By the way, I use this same system if I'm looking for a contractor to work on my own home. A contractor's business is not just swinging a hammer or sweating a pipe. They are in the communication business as well. There is nothing that bothers me more than a contractor that says he's going to do one thing and doesn't follow through. I want someone that I can communicate with, so if I'm looking for a contractor to do a particular job and I don't have a recommendation, I'm going to use this white paper to find a reliable contractor as well.

Susan: That is an easy way for me to pre-qualify an agent before I even meet them. It's another way for me to save time.

Kenny: It sure is. Just email me at **kenny@capeanninfo.com** and ask for my *13 Steps on How to Find a Really Effective Agent*. I'll get it right out to you.

There are also a number of questions that reference the marketing plans. "Do you use a stager, photographer, videographer?" "Will there be an individual property promotion website?" "How's the signage?" I'm happy to share all this.

What to Fix and What Not to Fix Before You Sell...

Susan: You mentioned earlier that lack of preparation is one of the biggest mistakes sellers make. How can I figure out what to fix and what not to fix before I sell? Based on your experience, what are your recommendations?

Kenny: I love to think like the buyer. It's key to get inside their heads and to think like they do.

When a buyer decides to come and look at your property, they have already vetted you thoroughly on the internet. They have looked at the photographs that were taken. They have looked at the video of your home. (You have real video, right?) They have looked at the assessor's records. They have looked at everything they can possibly find, before they make an appointment to come and view your property. Then they call their buyer's agent.

Most buyers are going to have an agent that they are working with. That agent is going to work in their best interests and help them get the property for the best price and terms. They make the appointment. When they show up to the appointment, they are interested in your house. It's not like the old days where buyers went across the threshold and that was the first time they saw the house. They may have looked at your house 10, 12, 15 times before they come across the threshold. So they are interested.

First, what are they going to be thinking about when they pull up in front of your house? You pull up in front of your house every night after work, and you are used to seeing it over and over and over again. That arborvitae at the corner of your house between your front door and your driveway was three feet tall when you planted it. Now it's 33 feet tall. You may not have noticed how big that arborvitae has gotten, but the buyer pulls up and says, "Wow! Where did that plant come from? It's blocking the view." The buyer may have a totally different view of your property than you have.

The second thing they think about when they pull up in front of your property is, "What are my friends and family going to think of the decision I made to buy this house? Are they going to think I made a good decision or bad decision?" They may not even be aware that that's what is going through their brain, but that is what's happening. "Are my friends and family going to think this is a good idea or a bad idea?" This is the way you need to be thinking when you are deciding what to fix and not to fix before you sell.

My overall bottom line for what to fix and not to fix is, if it looks like it needs to be fixed, you need to fix it or you need to get a price for it. The buyer is going to look at the item that needs to be fixed and double the price. Let's say for example, your property has a gas fired, hot water boiler that is 35 years old. The normal life expectancy is 25 years. It's running fine. You have maintained it, it runs great. That buyer, though, they know it's 35 years old because their home inspector is going to say, "This is like an old car. It will probably go for a lot longer. However, it may not. Think about replacing it now."

Automatically, the buyer thinks they need $15,000 for a new boiler where the new boiler may only cost $8,000. I'm not saying that you need to write a check to replace the boiler. What I'm saying is if you are not going to fix that black information hole that the boiler is in, you need to fill it, by getting an estimate. Have your plumber come in and write up an estimate for a new boiler, what it would take, so all of a sudden, the boiler that they think may need to be replaced for $15,000 is really only going to cost $8,000. That's the bottom line. What do we fix before we sell? You fix all the black holes or you fill them in by getting a price.

Susan: You're saying buyers will just naturally assume the worst unless we do something to remove the doubt.

Kenny: That's correct. They assume the worst and they double the price, because what they really want is the ability to negotiate a lower price. You totally take that away from them if you've already got a price on the work. "Oh my gosh, we need a new roof. That's a huge roof; it's going to be at least $20,000." It's often twice what it really costs. So if you've already got a bid that you can pass on, it totally disarms their way of thinking. Again. Preparation and anticipation.

The National Association of Realtors spends an enormous amount of money every year polling buyers and sellers; asking them questions. One of the things they put together is a report every January which details the return on investment for certain common household projects. I have copies of that report. If you'd like to see that report, I'd be happy to send it to you. It basically says if you spend X number of dollars to update a bathroom, it will take two years for you to break even on what you spent on the bathroom. The best ROI here in the Northeast, and it's different in different parts of the country, the best ROI here in the Northeast is the kitchen and or a bathroom remodel. You will typically break even and get your money back on the value of your home after about a year. The report is long and detailed and makes for interesting reading. If anyone would like a copy of the report, I'd be happy to send it to them. Just send me an email at kenny@capeanneinfo.com.

The Big Secret: How to Determine Who's Your Best Buyer...

Susan: So, the house is on the market now. We've done any necessary work to show it in the best way. The is interest in the property. How do I figure out who's going to buy my home?

Kenny: We call this "buyer profiling" and it's not something that is spoken of much by my colleagues. I'm not sure why, but we've had great success with our marketing when we profile. Once the property is ready for the market, we figure out who the buyer is going to be. We start off by looking at my seller client. Who is my seller client? What do they do for a living? How did they end up buying their home? Where did they come from? Where were they living prior to this? How many kids do they have or don't have? What do they do for recreation? Chances are the same type of person is going to buy the property when you're ready to sell.

The communities we work with here on Cape Ann are predominantly Manchester, Beverly, Gloucester, and Rockport. 25% of the properties are owned by folks who don't live here year round. These are second or third homes for them. Just by paying attention, we have narrowed down certain areas, certain towns here in Massachusetts, where people tend to move from to come here to Cape Ann and the North Shore. This is what I mean by profiling.

Susan: Ok, so I understand there are trends and profiles. How does this information help you sell my home?

Kenny: It allows me to target the right buyer. When preparing the marketing plan and putting together all the collateral, it allows me to key in on that particular person. If I have a property that is a three and a half bedroom beach house with a bath and a half, walking distance to the water, the people that own it now have owned it for 15 years, and they use it in the summertime, they don't use it in the wintertime, they get a seasonal tenant in there, chances are, that same type of person is going to want to buy that house. I'm going to look in their neighborhood and see where other buyers have come from and find the pattern. Those are the buyers that we're going after. It's just like solving a crime: if I can identify who's there now, then I can find the next owner. It's that simple.

Marketing Collateral: What to Use and Why...

Susan: I know from my own experience of looking for a home to buy, the marketing material on a property is very important. As a seller, what should I do, or not do, to market my home?

Kenny: Digital media is key today. Digital marketing, and by that, I mean websites and landing pages. It allows us to target the buyer.

Prior to putting a property on the internet, it needs to be prepared. The first time somebody sees your property, it's going to be about two inches wide by about two inches tall. It will be a little photograph on a website. That photograph needs to be set up and perfect. So we start with a stager. We stage just about everything we market.

I mentioned earlier that people like to buy model homes. Before we take any photographs, before we prepare any collateral, we have the stager come in and rearrange the furniture and/or bring in furniture to make it look like a model home. Then we use a professional still photographer to take those high resolution photographs and a professional videographer to take video of the house itself, as well as any interesting features about the house.

For example, if it's a 6-minute walk to the beach, I would want to do what is called a lifestyle video and have the photographer video the walk to the beach and what it's like to get from the house to the beach. If there is a boat ramp, let's take some video of the boat ramp. Let's show somebody rowing across the bay or getting into their kayak. Dogs make great actors in property videos so sometimes we have a cute dog running around the yard. We want to put as much "living" in the video as possible. And what's the point of video if it isn't moving??

We do all of this prior to putting the property on a website. Buyers don't go over the threshold until they've seen all the collateral. The number one way that people sort homes that they want to see is on the internet. When beginning their search, the number one first choice is the number of photographs. So we post as many photographs as possible. Here in Massachusetts, our Multiple Listing Service will allow us to put 30 photographs online for one house. You need to put at least 30 photographs up, as well as video if you want your property to be seen first before anyone else's. And they MUST be taken by a pro.

Pulling out your iPhone, or reusing some other snaps is simply not good enough these days because your competing against the other properties on the market. Everyone has upped their game, especially in this respect.

Susan: You mentioned there, 'beating the competition' is important to get buyers attention. What else can I do to market my property?

Kenny: Postcards, brochures, listing sheets and a showing book. Remember the profiling I talked about earlier? We have a specific neighborhood here in Gloucester that is a "beach home" neighborhood and populated predominantly by folks from a 6 or 8 town area between Rt 95 and Rt 2. If I have a property for sale in that beach neighborhood, the first thing we do is send a postcard with a beautiful photo of the house to people in those towns that fit the profile. That is targeted collateral.

We often do four-page, full color brochures that are mailed out in the same manner. It all depends on the property.

We also put together what's called a Home Book. Buyers want all the information possible on a property. They can get an awful lot of it on the internet but let's make it easier for them. Since it's all about how people feel, we obviously want to make them feel good, comfortable, so if we give them information instead of making them look for it, they feel good and we look good. Our Home Book is a way of putting all the pertinent data in one PDF file and making it available immediately.

Our Home Book will typically include the deed, the plot plan, an overhead shot, like a Google map or a Bing map. If it's a condominium, all the condominium documents are included, including the budgets. I will collect bills from my seller client and include those as well. How much is the landscaping every month? How much did they spend upgrading the kitchen? All this information is provenance, history of the property.

I can't tell you how many times a buyer has said to me at the end of the transaction, "You know when we first looked at this house, you sent us the Home Book and we loved it. There was so much information in there. It made us feel really, really comfortable doing business with you and the sellers." This is an important piece of marketing collateral and should always be part of the plan. We love the Home Book.

Susan: Is that something I would keep that in the house for buyers to look at? Or should I have many copies to give to all buyers or should I wait until the 'real buyer' stands up?

Kenny: We put one in the house and we also give it to each and every buyer's agent who calls on the property. As I mentioned, it's all about making people feel good. It's about making people look good, too. I have to work with the buyer's agent. I want to make it as easy for the buyer to say yes and I want to help the buyer's agent look good to their client. When the buyer's agent calls me to make an appointment to view the property, I follow up with an email confirming our conversation and appointment.

I also attach a copy of the Home Book. I say to them, "Oh, by the way, here is some extra information about the property that you and your client may find interesting. Feel free to share it with them." I don't put any of Sotheby's or Kenny MacCarthy branding on it so the buyer's agent will feel comfortable sharing it. They'll say, "Oh my gosh, this has just saved me so much work. I'm just going to hand this to my client." They get to pass it on to their client and say, "Look what I've got for you." The buyer's agent feels really good, the buyer feels really good, and I've made it easy for both of them to get to know the property and feel comfortable. Everybody is a winner.

Susan: That is quite brilliant. It really create the most likely scenario for them to be successful with my property!

Talk to me about online marketing. How do you recommend I take full advantage of what is available today?

Kenny: 99% of the properties available for sale will be found on Zillow, Trulia and Realtor.com. The most important thing that you can do as a seller is make sure the information those sites are displaying is correct. Your agent should know how to manipulate those websites. We have accounts at all three. We put individual photographs up on all three. Those are the three major conduits where your property will be seen over and over again. It's just very important that the information shown on those sites is correct. Here in MA, those sites download from MLS PIN.

We also use what is called a property-specific website. Before we begin our marketing, we buy a domain name that matches the property address. If the property, for example, is 74 Grapevine Road in Gloucester, we will purchase 74grapevinerd.com and print a sign saying "74grapevinerd.com" that goes over the "for sale" sign. It points buyers to the website. The reasoning behind this is simple: if someone is driving by and interested, I want to get as much information into their hands as possible. Most buyers have smart phones. They see the sign rider, they pull up next to the house, they are interested in the house, all they have to do is go to their web browser and type in www.74grapevinerd.com for example and it brings them to a website that speaks only to that particular property.

On that website, they will be able to see the professional photographs and video. They will be able to get a copy of the Home Book right then and there if they want it. All of the information is in one place on that website.

Susan: You do that for every home that you sell?

Kenny: Yes, we do; single family and condos, everything we market.

Susan: I guess the bottom line here is to work with a pro, an agent that knows what they're doing, especially online. You do an awful lot above and beyond your typical agent.

Kenny: Thanks for noticing. There's a lot to it. Technology is an ever changing landscape. We put a lot of time in keeping up with it. Our clients don't have to stay up to speed, that's what we get paid for. It's our job.

Accurate Pricing: The 5-7-10 Rule...

Susan: We spoke earlier about how much my home is worth, but that is a little different than whether it's priced correctly to attract buyers and get the best price for me.

How do I know if I'm pricing my home correctly?

Kenny: I have a rule called the 5-7-10 Rule. And it rarely fails. Picture this: water up against a dam. The water represents interested buyers waiting for a particular property and the dam is holding them back until the property is available. When the property comes on the market and is available for sale, the dam breaks and we get an immediate rush of interested buyers. If the property is presented properly and priced properly, we will have at least 5 to 7 showings in the first 10 days of market time. If we don't have at least 5 to 7 showings in the first 10 days, then the property pricing is off by 7% to 10%. I've been tracking this for more than 10 years and it hasn't failed yet.

The second part of the rule is that we should have one offer for every 5 to 7 showings if we're priced within the buyer's value range. If there are 5 to 7 showings in the first 10 days and no offers, the buyers' perception is that the pricing is too far off to attempt to negotiate so they walk away. Remember, earlier in our conversation, I said that when buyers get to the property, they've already vetted it thoroughly. The only thing they haven't done is gone across the threshold to see the property in person. By the time the buyer gets to one of my properties, they know everything about it except for how it feels. So when they get there, they are VERY interested. They've got a check book with them. They just want to see how it feels, how it smells, how it sounds. That's why I can say with confidence, and my 10 years of tracking helps, too, that every 5 to 7 "over the threshold showings," we're going to get an offer. If we don't, then I know our pricing is off by 7% to 10%. That's the 5-7-10 Rule.

Susan: If I'm not getting the showings after 10 days, do you recommend reducing the price at that point, or do you wait a certain number of days?

Kenny: We usually wait a couple of weeks, and we go by the feedback we get from the other agents. After 10 days to 2 weeks, we re-evaluate, check the pricing feedback that we are getting, and go from there.

The greatest thing about digital marketing is that we can always track how many people have seen a property online. If I'm getting a hundred hits on the website, but no one is calling to see it, there is something very wrong. If I'm getting a hundred hits on the website and 10 people have seen it, and I haven't got an offer, something is very wrong.

The only time people won't look at it or won't make an offer is if they don't think that the price is within a negotiable distance. A negotiable distance is 3-5%. That's why I say, if they are not making offers, then the price is off 7-10%.

The Best Negotiating Strategy for Low Ball Offers...

Susan: Low ball offers can be frustrating as a seller, and it's easy to think of them as a waste of time. What is your advice on handling low ball offers? Should I just reject them outright?

Kenny: As a seller, remember what you're trying to accomplish. Get the best price and terms possible, right? You've prepared your property; you've chosen an agent to help you market it. You have great photographs and great video and websites. You've determined the launch price and put it on the market for sale. That price is almost always going to be at the upper edge of the pricing envelope. We don't want to leave any money on the table. That's your job. That's my job, too, if I'm representing you.

The buyer's job is 180 degrees the other way. The buyer's job is to try and steal it. The last thing a buyer wants to do is pay too much. They don't want to regret their decision. They don't want to look stupid. Their job is to try and steal it from you. Low ball offers are just the buyer doing their job: offering a price at the bottom edge of the pricing envelope. Just like you don't want to leave any money on the table, the buyer doesn't want to pay more than he/she has to.

If they've stepped across your threshold, they're really interested. They've taken the time and effort to vet it online, make an appointment with their agent, get in their car, and come see your property. They are interested. I don't care what the offer is, that offer indicates desire and, as such, needs to be treated with respect. I don't care how low it is. If a buyer puts pen to paper, work it.

I can't tell you how many times we've started with a "low ball" offer and then got the buyer to within 3% of our asking price and made the sale happen. Don't forget, the buyer is petrified of paying too much. Their biggest fear is that they make you an offer and you say, "OK. I'll take your offer," because, they automatically think that if you accept their offer, they might have been able to get it for less.

How many times have you purchased something, offered a certain amount of money for a car, for example, and the person said, "OK, I'll take it." Then you said to yourself, "Ugh, no negotiating. I paid too much. I could have got it for less." Same situation here, unless the property has just come on the market and is really special so they make a full-price offer, they are going to offer less and try to negotiate.

That's when we go to work and "work" the offer. It starts with learning as much as possible about the buyer's agent and the buyer and their circumstances. I could spend days talking about negotiating scenarios. It's one of the most important services we perform because our success is measured precisely in dollars. We're trained and tweaking our skills constantly.

I will mention this: one of the things that we do while negotiating is to send a letter with the counteroffer that explains our terms, our motivation. Giving the buyer a little insight and making my seller client "a real person" works wonders. Here's an example: we have a $750,000 property and the buyer makes an offer of $600,000. We're going to write a letter back, justifying why we believe our property is worth $750,000. We tell them that we're willing to counter at $745,000 to show a willingness to negotiate. Then we wait and hear what they say. We don't just arbitrarily drop the price. Always give a reason. That is a key negotiating tenet. Don't just lower the price. Give a reason.

Back to your original question, what do I do with a low ball offer? We always counter it.

Next Steps...

Susan: There are many great ideas here Kenny. Just in the time we've had, I think you've helped people make or save thousands of dollars from their home.

If someone reading this is interested in listing their North Shore home, how can they get in touch with you to talk about the best next steps?

Kenny: I'm always happy for people to call me. My phone number is **(978) 758-0983**. You can also email at **kenny@nshoremove.com**.

If you'd like to take a look at some of the videos I've posted talking about buying and selling on the North Shore, you can find them at **youtube.com/kennymaccarthy**.

Susan: I want to thank you for your time today Kenny. It has been very enlightening to see some of the thought process a top agent goes through to successfully sell a home on the North Shore..

Kenny: You are welcome. It's been my pleasure. I love my job and love talking about it.

The Systems and Strategies for Maximum Results...

You've been thinking about it for a long time and know that selling your home is a lot of work. You're anxious, worrying about giving it away or, even worse, not being able to sell it at all!

That's where we come in. We help people just like you use systems and strategies to sell their home for maximum results.

> **Step 1**: We begin with the end in mind, using Market Profiling to determine who your buyer will be. Who's most likely to want to buy your home? Profiling is absolutely key for success in marketing your home.
>
> **Step 2**: We do a room by room analysis using our Maximum Home Value Audit and make experienced recommendations to best showcase your home.
>
> **Step 3**: We will help you to determine the maximum price your buyer will pay in today's market by creating a pinpoint pricing analysis.
>
> **Step 4**: We take it from there and market your property - using the other steps in our exclusive 7-Step Marketing Plan, including staging, professional photography, captivating video, promotion and the power of social media. We also utilize the exclusive marketing agreements we have with WSJ, NY Times, Architectural Digest and other media.

Waiting for the right buyer can take forever. Using our Systems and Strategies, finding the right buyer to pay the right price in the right time frame is a systematized result.

If you'd like us to help, simply call me on **(978) 758-0983** or email **kenny@nshoremove.com** and we'll take it from there.

About the Author

Kenny MacCarthy has been a full time, career, residential real estate professional on the North Shore and Cape Ann since 1994. As a trained negotiator and "problem anticipator", he guides his clients with expert, first-hand knowledge that translates into prescient advice. Many say the detailed consultations with him prior to making their decisions were the keys to their success.

Experience allows Kenny to completely represent the needs of his clients. He always acts in a fiduciary capacity, providing sound, confidential and discrete advice that yields predictable results.

The internet has made the world smaller and more interconnected, giving buyers and sellers all the information they want, when they want it. The ability to harness this technology is one of Kenny's unique abilities. He has led his field with speed, agility and a broad reach by developing real estate specific applications that enable him to achieve his clients' goals. Online as kennymaccarthy.com since 1998, with over 450 YouTube videos to his credit, Kenny's peers awarded him "Innovative Marketer of the Year" in the fall of 2013.

An avid hiker, Kenny is often found on the trails of Ravenswood, the White Mountains, Mt. Rainier, the Grand Canyon, Coyote Gulch Utah or Sagamartha Park, Nepal. Sometimes Kit, the mutt, goes with him.